1

STUDY THE BIBLE

Study the Bible with friend & neighbor—an evangelism and discipleship tool.

TABLE OF CONTENTS

INSTRUCTIONS 6

1. IS THERE A GOD? 8

2. WHO IS GOD? 11

3. WHAT GOD WANTS...14

4. IS THE BIBLE RELIABLE? 17

5. HUMANKIND 22

6. THE PERSON OF JESUS 26

7. THE WORK OF JESUS 29

8. SALVATION 33

9. REPENTANCE 36

10. THE HOLY SPIRIT 40

11. BAPTISM 44

12. THE CHURCH 48

13. CHURCH MEMBERSHIP 53

14. CHRISTIAN OBEDIENCE 56

15. PRAYER..60

16. EVANGELISM 64

17. CONTINUED SPIRITUAL GROWTH........................68

18. HOW TO READ THE BIBLE.................................72

INSTRUCTIONS

This book is intended to have a leader take a student through the scriptures to point them to the reality of God, the need to follow Jesus, the need to be involved in the church, and the essentials of our faith and Christian disciplines that allow a person to live a Christian life.

You can begin this study with literally anyone, whether they are a Christian or not. At certain points, it will become obvious that it's time to make a decision: to follow Jesus, to repent of sins, to get baptized, to join the church, etc. If the person is not ready, you can decide to finish the study, pause the study, or go back and revisit previous lessons, as is appropriate for the situation.

As a leader, it will help if you have a solid understanding of the passages before you take someone through the materials. The best way to do that is to go through it with someone else first.

A piece of advice: Don't skip the practicums. Jesus taught his disciples and then sent them out to do the work. The point of this study is to train up Christians who live authentic lives as followers of Jesus. They will need to know how to do the good works that God set aside for us before creation. The practicums will make that possible.

Encourage preparation so that you can discuss the passages without having to look up every verse. As a leader, you should always prepare by looking up the verses ahead of time and reading the leader notes at the end of each chapter.

Don't feel pressure to finish a whole chapter every meeting. They are arranged topically, and not meant to be rushed. Pray your student through the materials and see what God does for his kingdom and glory!

1. Is There a God?

Purpose: To determine whether or not it is rational to believe in God at all.

Arguments from Existence

Because the universe exists there must be a creator (cosmological). Just as a product such as a watch is evidence of a producer, a watchmaker, the reality of existence proves there is a transcendent creator (teleological). Further, the fact that we can imagine a being so sovereign and supreme as God is evidence that such a God must exist – otherwise from whose imagination did this God come to be (Ontological)?

The second law of thermodynamics states that the total entropy of an isolated system can never increase or decrease over time. In other words, there is a particular amount of matter and energy in the universe and it never changes or grows or decreases—it only changes form within the universe. The question is, if nature does not allow for a system to increase or decrease, then how did the cosmos come to be in the first place? It requires a creator that's supremacy extends beyond the laws of nature—i.e. a god.

Read Genesis 1:1, John 1:1-4, Colossians 1:16-18. In what ways does the Bible reflect or conflict with what philosophy teaches about the existence of the universe?

Argument from Morality

The moral argument suggests that the widespread agreement on primary moral issues (such as the evil or murder) is evidence of intelligent design.

Read Romans 2:14-15 and discuss the ways that the Bible confirms or conflicts with the Moral Argument for God.

Experiential (Presuppositional)

When someone becomes a Christian and they are filled with the Holy Spirit, they have an experience of faith that becomes a testimony of the truths the scriptures teach. In this way a Christian can presuppose the truths of the scriptures when they talk to other people about the existence of God. Consider what the scriptures teach about the existence of God.

- What do all people know about God from observing the creation? (Romans 1:19-20)
- What do all people know about God's righteous standards? (Romans 1:18)
- Why don't all people believe in God? (Romans 1:21)

9

- Why do people who are not Christians have a hard time understanding or submitting to the Bible's teaching about God? (1 Corinthians 2:14)

Further Reading

- Creation (Genesis 1)
- Power of experience and testimony (Acts 1:3)
- The foolishness of disbelief (Psalm 14:1)
- Defending the faith (1 Peter 3:15)
- The unbelieving (Proverbs 26:4-5)
- Believing in God is not enough (Hebrews 11:6)
- Faith (Hebrews 11:1)

Leader Notes

Leaders should look up the various philosophical arguments on the internet and make sure to understand the basics of each. Also, read up on presuppositional apologetics and be prepared to talk about any/all scriptures in the lesson. Ask questions from pastors or others who can help prepare you to teach the material.

2. WHO IS GOD?

Purpose: To explore who God is according to the Bible.

God

There is one true God (1 Timothy 1:17).

What is God like?

- Creator (Nehemiah 9:6)
- Holy (Leviticus 11:44)
- Sustainer (Colossians 1:17)
- Ruler (Psalm 22:28)
- Infinite (Revelation 1:18)
- All Powerful (Jeremiah 32:17)
- All Knowing (1 John 3:20)

The Trinity

The eternal triune God reveals Himself to us as Father, Son, and Holy Spirit, with distinct personal attributes, but without division of nature, essence, or being.

- God's Oneness (Deuteronomy 4:35,39; Deuteronomy 6:4; Isaiah 46:9; 1 Corinthians 8:5–6; James 2:19)

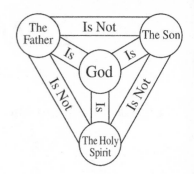

- Trinitarian Formula (Matthew 28:19; 2 Corinthians 13:14; Ephesians 1:17)

The Father

The Father is an uncreated, eternal spirit. All life comes from God, the Father. God has determined the timing of all of his purposes according to his authority. (John 4:24, John 5:26, Acts 1:7)

The Son

Jesus Christ is the eternal Son of God. Jesus is fully God and also fully human. Jesus acts as high priest of God on behalf of humanity. Jesus sat down at the right hand of the Father in heaven where he rules God's Kingdom. Jesus is the one who makes it possible for humans to become children of God. (Colossians 2:9, Romans 1:3-4; Hebrews 4:14; Mark 16:19; Galatians 4:4-5)

The Spirit

The Spirit of God is the power of God in this world. He convicts of sins, draws people to the Father, and empowers followers of Christ to carry out God's purposes. (John 16:8; John 6:44; 1 Corinthians 12:11)

Leader Notes

Leaders should begin with a general discussion about who the student thinks God is. Use the internet to get an understanding of who people of other religions say God is. Look up 'Moralistic Therapeutic Deism' and make note for yourself that many people see God as merely a being who wants people to be good (moralistic), who is there whenever you need to call on him (therapeutic), and who leaves us alone to live our lives unless we need him (deism). This will help you to highlight the personal nature of God, that he wants an authentic, purposeful, and eternal relationship with the humans he has created.

Further, the trinity is a difficult doctrine. The student will not likely come to a full understanding of the trinity from this study. What they must understand is that Christians believe God to be a singular God who is spoken of in the scriptures in three distinct persons. They are distinct and yet one—note the diagram. Ask questions from pastors or others who can help prepare you to teach the material.

3. WHAT GOD WANTS

Purpose: To demonstrate that God wants people to be His children—God wants a family.

Your Father by Nature

We are born into the Kingdom of the world and by nature children of the devil. He is the ruler of this world and has authority over it. Our sin, disobedience, deceit, and treachery demonstrate that we are by nature children of the devil.

- The Devil (John 8:44)
- Ruler of the Air (Ephesians 2:1-3)
- Authority (Luke 4:6)
- Sins (1 John 3:8)
- Weeds (Matthew 13:37-39)
- Deceit and Treachery (Acts 13:10)

Adoption as Sons (and Daughters)

If you believe in Jesus, God has predestined you to be adopted as a child of God! He has placed His Spirit in you so that you receive a new nature, a redeemed nature and you are able to love your heavenly Father. Those who love their Father are not content in sin but imitate God. Our Father disciplines us through suffering so that we grow and mature and conform to the image of Christ.

- Sons of God (Galatians 4:4-6)
- Those who Believe (1 John 1:12)
- Spirit (Romans 8:15)
- Peacemakers (Matthew 5:9)
- Redemption (Romans 8:23)
- Sin (1 John 3:9)
- Imitators (Ephesians 5:1)
- Assurance (1 John 5:1)
- Suffering (Hebrews 12:10)
- Predestination (Ephesians 1:5)
- Conformity (Romans 8:29)

Fatherhood of God

Read the parable of the Prodigal Son (Luke 15:11-32). A parable is an imaginative story that represents realities of the Kingdom of God. The characters and events are illustrations of actual realities.

- Who is the Father?
- Who is the younger son who demands his inheritance?
- Who do you think the pig farmer represents?
- When the younger son takes his inheritance whose son is he living like?
- What does the younger son have before his rebellion?

- What position did the younger son hope he could receive in returning to his Father?
- How does the Father treat the younger son when he returns from his rebellion?

Introspection

Remembering the story of the Prodigal Son, how does your story mirror the parable?

- Who are you by nature?
- How have you rebelled against God the Father? How have you squandered the wealth He has given you?
- When we return to our Father, how does He receive us? As lowly servants? As sons? As heirs?

Leader Notes

Leaders should take their time going over the verses in the lesson. Make sure to have a discussion about the prodigal son and supplement this part of the lesson with any other scriptures or ideas that remind you that God is a personal God, who wants us as a family, not simply as obedient servants. A future study could be done using "What Does God Want?"

4. Is the Bible Reliable?

Purpose: To demonstrate the reliability of the Bible, its authenticity, and the need to base our understanding of God and Christianity on the Bible.

The Bible

The Bible is the primary source material that frames and directs the religion of Christianity. The word used in the Bible to refer to itself is *scripture*. Historically, Christian preaching and theology has been done form the Bible. You can see this in the way the New Testament authors reference the Old Testament. New Testament authors often use the phrases "God says" and "the Holy Spirit says" when they reference Old Testament passages or ideas. For the New Testament authors, Scripture is the record of God speaking and revealing Himself to His people.

The NT writers describe scripture as "strongly confirmed" (2 Pet. 1:19), trustworthy "deserving of full acceptance" (1 Tim. 1:15), and "confirmed" (Heb. 2:3). Its word "endures forever" (1 Pet. 1:24–25). Those who build their lives on Scripture "will not be put to shame" (Rom. 9:33). The Bible was written for "instruction" and "encouragement" (Rom. 15:4), to lead to "salvation through faith" (2 Tim. 3:15), to guide people toward godliness (2 Tim. 3:16), and to equip believers for good works (2 Tim. 3:17).

The purpose of the Bible is to place men and women in right standing before God and to enable Christians to seek God's glory in all of life's activities and efforts. It is above all a story about God redeeming people who have sinned against him.

Reliability

It is common today for people to be critical of the Bible because the writings are ancient. How can you know that this is what was originally written? The reality is, we have more assurance that the Bible is accurate to its original than any other ancient writing on the planet.

Compare the New Testament to the Greek historian Herodotus. We have 8 copies of his work, the oldest dating to 1300 years after the original was written. This is considered reliable as historical record. There are more than 5500 copies of the New Testament, the oldest dating to less than 100 years after the originals.

The closest ancient manuscript to the New Testament is the Iliad written by Homer in 900 BC. Here are 643 copies of the Iliad, the oldest being 500 years after the original. Textual critics recognize 95% accuracy between these texts to the original. That's impressive, but again, there are over 5500 copies of the New Testament, the oldest dating to less than 100 years after the originals, and textual critics recognize the New Testament documents as being 99.5% accurate to the original. In fact, of the discrepancies between the most ancient New Testament manuscripts, there is not a single discrepancy that effects Christian doctrine in any significant way.

For many years, scholars have agreed on the reliability of the New Testament but argued about the Old Testament as the oldest copies of the Hebrew Old Testament were from the approximately 980 AD. That's a huge gap from the originals. However, in 1947 when the texts called the Dead Sea Scrolls were discovered in caves in Qumran, many far more ancient manuscripts were discovered. The most significant were two copies of the book of Isaiah. When they were compared to the contemporary copies of Isaiah, they proved to be 95% accurate. Even at that, the 5% discrepancies were made up of spelling errors and ink splats and slips which introduced absolutely no challenge to the meaning of the text.

Authorship

The Bible is not only a divine book but also a human book. It is important to recognize that the biblical writers wrote down God's message through the lens of their own ideas, beliefs, and linguistic resources. They wrote to specific people with particular needs at particular times and the text reflects that context. The human authors were not puppets who were lifted out of their culture, rather, the text reflects the cultural nuances of the human authors.

The protestant Bible consists of 66 books written by over 40 authors spanning almost 1,500 years so there are many human contexts to consider. In spite of the variance in context, the Bible reveals to

God's people the unifying story of His redeeming words and acts. The ultimate focus of the Bible is the person and work of Jesus Christ.

The Bible Testifies About Itself

Repeatedly the New Testament affirms the authority of the Old Testament scriptures. The earliest disciples and likewise the early church was built on the foundation of Jesus Christ as He has been revealed throughout history in the ancient Hebrew texts we call the Old Testament.

- Purpose (1 Timothy 3:16-17)
- Human and Divine Authorship (2 Peter 1:20-21)
- Sustainability (John 10:35)
- Revelation of the Good News (Acts 8:35)
- Reasoning (Acts 18:28)
- A Testimony of Redemptive History (Luke 24:27)

New Testament Authority

The New Testament was written by the Apostles and early Disciples who were appointed by Christ. The New Testament doesn't affirm the New Testament for obvious reason, but it does affirm the authority of the New Testament authors. Early church documents and church history affirm that the books of the New Testament have been considered reliable since their authorship. Even letters to specific churches and people were considered to be authoritative and circulated among the churches (Colossians 4:16).

- Appointed by Jesus (Mark 3:14)
- Authority (Mark 6:7)
- Preaching (Mark 6:12)
- Teachers (Acts 2:42)
- Power (Acts 4:33)
- First in Authority (1 Corinthians 12:28)
- Honesty (1 Timothy 2:7)

Leader Notes

Leaders should be prepared to answer questions about the reliability of the Old and New Testament. Leaders should review the history and canonicity of the Bible as that will likely come up during this study. More educated people may be interested in the topic of textual criticism. Also, leader should be prepared to answer questions as to why they personally find the Bible reliable.

5. HUMANKIND

Purpose: To understand who humans are on a fundamental level.

Who Are Humans?

Humans are a special and unique part of creation, set apart from the angelic beings and set apart from the rest of creations. Humans are described as wonderful, unique, valuable, and beautiful in God's eyes and were uniquely crafted to carry out God's purposes on the earth.

- God's Wonderful Creation (Psalm 139:13-16)
- Unique Creatures (Isaiah 13:12)
- God's Workers on the Earth (Genesis 1:28, Ephesians 2:10)
- "Clay" (Isaiah 64:8)
- Valuable (Matthew 10:29-31)
- Designed for Beauty (Ecclesiastes 3:11)

Imagers

Humans were created to image God, created in His likeness. But sin and disobedience to God defiled the image of God on humankind.

- Image/Likeness (Genesis 1:26-27)
- Image defiled (Romans 1:22-23)
- Image Descendancy (Genesis 5:3)
- Graven Images (Exodus 34:17)
- Partial Imagers (Romans 8:29, Colossians 3:10)
- Restoring the Image (Ephesians 4:24)
- Perfect Image of God (Colossians 1:15)
- Image Fully Restored (Philippians 1:6)

Consider the reality and nature of Jesus, the perfect image of God. In what ways are all people still partial imagers of God? In what ways do we need to grow to image God more? When will we finally image God perfectly like Adam did in the garden and like Jesus does? What do you think that will be like?

In Sin

Most believe we are born morally ambiguous and that, at some point in the person's maturity, they make choices that either make them a good or bad person. The scriptures teach something different. The scriptures teach that people are born into the Kingdom of the World (remember, where your father is the devil) and that you must be adopted as a child of God where you are given a new and better nature. The nature of humans by birth is that of a sinner, in need of redemption.

- Sin as Moral Grievance (Genesis 4:4-7, James 4:17)
- Scope of Sin (Romans 3:23)
- Obviousness of Sin (Galatians 5:19-21)
- Earthly Nature of Sin (Colossians 3:5-6)
- Comprehensiveness of Sin (Isaiah 64:6, Romans 3:12)
- Enemies of God (James 4:4)
- Pleasing God (Romans 8:8)
- Source of Sin (James 1:13-18)
- Why God Allows Sin to Continue (Galatians 3:22)   \
- God's Wrath for Sin (Romans 1:18)
- Responsibility for Sin (Romans 1:20)
- Commonality (1 Corinthians 10:13)
- Deception to Sin (Matthew 6:13, Luke 4:13,1 Peter 5:8)
- Sin's Grasp (John 8:34)

Leader Notes

Leaders should be careful to emphasize the reality that humans are a wonderful part of God's creation. We have sinned and fallen short of God's glory, but God is not done with us. He loves humankind and continues to work to carry out His purposes through us. It is easy to fall to fatalistic thinking, that humankind is not worth saving, that a particular individual may not be able to be saved, or something like that. But God is a great redeemer and still has amazing things in store for humanity.

In talking about imaging, use discernment if you want to talk about abortion, suicide, euthanasia, war, and other difficult topics of that sort. Every human is a partial and potential imager of God, valued and loved by Him, and we must not take lightly any such topic of debate.

6. THE PERSON OF JESUS

Purpose: To understand the nature of Jesus, his eternality and Lordship.

Eternal

Jesus is also eternal, which means he is not just a god, but the one true God. He was before all things, the first and the last, the eternal Word that never changes. He exists eternally as a High Priest for his people.

- Before All Things (Colossians 1:17)
- Unchanging (Hebrews 13:8)
- First and Last (Revelation 1:17)
- Eternal Word of Life (1 John 1:1)
- Eternal Priesthood (Hebrews 7:28)
- I AM (John 8:58)

Divine

Jesus is divine. He is God, the 2nd member of the trinity. He is the Word of God in flesh, equal with the Father. All deity is in Him; Jesus is lacking in nothing that would be required to be the supreme God. Before coming to earth, he was in the form of God and He sat on God's eternal throne. He is worthy of worship only with the Father and Spirit.

- Word (John 1.1)
- Equality with the Father (John 5:18)
- All Deity (Colossians 2:9)
- Form of God (Philippians 2:5-6)
- Eternal Throne (Hebrews 1:8)
- Worship (Matthew 2:11, 14:33)

Human

Jesus was also human. Read about his birth in Luke 2:1-20. He is the Word of God in flesh. He emptied himself of his divine essence when he came to earth as a human. He had a human will and matured as humans do. He came in the flesh and was recognized as people, in every way, as a man.

- Word in Flesh (John 1.1,14)
- Emptying (Philippians 2:7-8)
- Will (Luke 22:42)
- Maturity (Luke 2:52)
- Come in Flesh (1 John 4:2-3)
- The Man (1 Timothy 2:5)

LORD

When the biblical authors referred to Jesus as, "Lord Jesus," they
had more in mind than that He is their master or lord. In their mind,
they were connecting Jesus with the LORD of the Old Testament
who walked with Adam and Even in the Garden of Eden story and
who appeared to the Hebrew people throughout the Old
Testament narratives. Consider these statements and who the
Bible's authors believed Jesus to be.

- Lord (Adonai) GOD (Yahweh) (Amos 3:8)
- The LORD God in Flesh (Genesis 3:8)
- Who Jesus thought He was (Matthew 7:22, Luke 6:46)
- Jesus in Joel (Acts 2:21-22 [Lord], cf. Joel 2:32 [LORD])

Leader Notes

Leaders should be comfortable defending Jesus' divinity and
humanity but should be leery of trying to create an analogy for this
biblical reality. Jesus is both 100% God and 100% human as taught
by the scriptures and these facts are often underplayed by
imperfect analogies.

The leader should also be comfortable talking about Jesus as the
Lord of the Old Testament. Where and how do you see Jesus in the
Old Testament?

7. THE WORK OF JESUS

Purpose: To review the story of Jesus's death and resurrection and to discuss the ways in which his death and resurrection result in the redemption of people and the whole of creation.

The Story

Read the story of Jesus's betrayal and death in Luke 22-24. It's easy to miss the significance of Jesus's death and why he had to die, especially if he was just going to come back to life anyway. The narrative begins with the religious leaders' plot to kill Jesus because the common people loved and followed Jesus more than them. Satan possessed one of the disciples named Judas and Judas betrayed Jesus to the Jewish leaders. The story comes to a climax when Jesus is hung on a cross, a horrific way to die.

Notice the quick exchange Jesus has with the criminals on the cross. One of them mocks Jesus, but the other repents of his sins and defends Jesus. Jesus makes a promise to him that he will join him in Paradise. This reminds us that the good news about Jesus that gives us redemption can be very simple, but the significance of the events of the cross and resurrection are also deep and profoundly philosophical.

Regeneration

Regeneration is an act of the Holy Spirit where the disposition of the soul is made holy through the belief of an individual in the truth of God's word, and where the exercise of holiness is made possible in the life of a person.

- Regeneration (Titus 3:5)
- Born Again (John 3:3)
- Practice of Sin (1 John 3:9)
- New Creation (2 Corinthians 5:17)
- Spiritually Alive (Colossians 2:13)
- Purified (1 Peter 1:23)

Justification

Justification is the judicial act of God in which He declares a person righteous according to their faith and the person is acquitted of their sins against God and his creation.

- By Faith not Law (Romans 3:28, Galatians 2:16)
- Peace with God (Romans 5:1)
- Justified by Christ's Blood (Romans 3:25–26)
- Works (James 2:21-24)
- Lowliness (1 Corinthians 1:28-29)
- Attributed Righteousness (Genesis 15:6)

Sanctification

Sanctification is the continuing work of the Holy Spirit in the life of a believer, where the holy disposition that occurs during Regeneration is strengthened and maintained. NOTE: Justification is declared righteousness; sanctification is the process of becoming actually righteous.

- Living by Christ (Galatians 2:20)
- By Truth (John 17:17)
- God's Will (1 Thessalonians 4:3–5)
- By Christ's Death (Hebrews 10:14, 13:12)
- Promise of (Philippians 1:6)
- Partaking in the Divine Nature (2 Peter 1:2-4)

Glorification

Glorification is the completed act of sanctification where the believer has become, through the power of the Holy Spirit, actually righteous. This is a work that is not completed until the end.

- Completely Sanctified (1 Thessalonians 5:23)
- At Christ's Return (Colossians 3:4)
- Product of Justification and Sanctification (Romans 8:30)
- Eternal Inheritance (1 Peter 1:3–5)
- Blameless in the End (1 Corinthians 1:6–8)
- Reconciled by Blood (Colossians 1:22)

All Things New

The curse of sin is comprehensive, reaching beyond humankind to the earth and the cosmos. The glorification that the Christian awaits is the same glorification that the rest of creation waits for as well. In the end, Jesus makes all things new.

- New Cosmos and Earth (Revelation 21:1)
- New Holy City/Temple (Revelation 21:2)
- God Dwells with His Family (Revelation 21:3)
- Promised Relief (Isaiah 30:19)
- No More Pain (Revelation 21:4)
- Promised New Creation (Isaiah 65:17-19)
- All Things Made New (Revelation 21:5)
- Eternal Perfection (Revelation 21:6)

Leader Notes

The leader should be ready to speak about the different elements of the Gospel message. How does Jesus' death on the cross result in justification, regeneration, and sanctification? What is the nature of the eternal state? Be ready to talk about what it means to actually be perfected, to live eternally with Jesus, and review the physical aspects of the eternal Kingdom.

8. SALVATION

Purpose: To demonstrate what it is that Christians are saved from and what they are saved to and for, as well as to clarify who actually receives salvation.

Who is Saved?

Those who believe in Jesus, have faith in him and his work on the cross, and who are loyal to the Kingdom of God over the Kingdom of the World are saved.

- Believe (John 3:16)
- Through Faith (Ephesians 2:8-9)
- Confession of Lordship (Romans 10:9)
- Fruit (Matthew 7:16)
- Love for One Another (John 13:35)
- Demonstrated Loyalty (James 2:14)

From What

We are saved from the wrath of God that is due us for our sins. What the Bible calls 'hell' is an eternal separation from God and everything that is good.

- Wrath (Romans 2:5)

- Spiritual Death (Romans 6:23)

- Enmity with God (Romans 5:10)

- Destruction (Matthew 10:28)

- Condemnation (Romans 8:1)

- Eternal Punishment (2 Thessalonians 1:9a)

- Separation from God (2 Thessalonians 1:9b)

To What

We are saved first and foremost to Christ—we believe in Jesus to get Jesus. This means that we are able to enter into the presence of God by Jesus Christ's righteousness. This is a present reality through the indwelling Holy Spirit and an eternal physical reality.

- Eternal Life (John 3:36)

- Eternal Perfection (Philippians 3:12)

- God's Kingdom (James 2:5)

- God's Family (Romans 8:29)

For What

We are not saved by good works, but because we are saved, we should perform good works, namely that we would be God's agents to proclaim the good news about Jesus, organize and educate His disciples, and participate in the world as representatives of God's perfect, eternal Kingdom.

- Righteousness (Titus 2:11-12)
- Thankfulness (Colossians 2:6-7)
- Good Works (Ephesians 2:10)
- Fellowship and Community (Hebrews 10:23-25)

Leader Notes

At this point the leader needs to be ready to ask hard questions. What does the student believe exactly? Do they believe what is required to be saved? Does their life demonstrate the reality of their salvation? If there are questions, this is a great time to deal with those before moving on. Take your time if need be and pray with the individual for faith and repentance if it has not become a conviction yet.

Make sure to highlight how awful existence apart from God is, but really focus on how wonderful life with God is and will be eternally. Encourage them to see the importance of righteousness, good works, faithfulness, and fellowship with God's people as shadows of our eternal joy.

9. REPENTANCE

Purpose: To demonstrate the importance of repentance in the life of the Christian and in the Kingdom of God.

What is Repentance?

To repent is to turn away from your sins. The Christian learns to hate sin and love righteousness. Repentance is the retraining of your habits, behaviors, and attitudes to love what God loves and to live as Christ lives.

- Turn from sin (2 Chronicles 7:14)
- Turning from wickedness (Acts 8:22)
- Purification (James 4:8)
- Secret sin (Proverbs 28:13)
- Heart issue (Romans 2:5)
- Commanded (Matthew 4:17)

How to Repent of Sins

Repentance is not something you simply do. Certainly, you must take responsibility for your sin and be intentional about repenting of sins. But repentance is a change of heart that cause you to grieve your sins. Repentance comes from God and, thus, part of repentance is confessing your sins to God.

- God gives it (Acts 5:31, 11:18; 2 Timothy 2:25)
- Rely on God's Leading (Romans 2:4)
- Take responsibility (Acts 17:30)
- Be intentional (Matthew 3:8)
- Confess your sins (Psalm 38:18)
- Grieve your sins (2 Corinthians 7:9-10)

Repentance and Salvation

Repentance is tied up in salvation. Many people, for fear of sounding as if we merit our salvation by our good works, have emphasized that God's grace is so free that repentance is not part of the equation. But we are called to turn from our sin and turn to God. We are told that God is waiting for us to come to repentance, a clear illusion to salvation. When we express a heart of repentance through confession, God grants us forgiveness of sins. When sinners repent, the heavens rejoice, for repentance marks authentic, saving belief. Because repentance comes from God ultimately, it is tied up in Regeneration.

- Turning to God (Acts 3:19)
- Patience (2 Peter 3:9)
- Rejoicing in Heaven (Luke 15:7)

- Confession (1 John 1:9)

- Repentance and Belief (Mark 1:15)

- Ordering (2 Corinthians 7:10)

Repentance and Accountability Practicum

The Christian must be concerned with sin. Whether you have been a Christian for a long time, or you are new in the faith, create a detailed list of the sins you struggle with on a regular basis. Be specific. Cite examples of times when you have fallen to this sin. Take note of people who your sin has hurt.

Next, go to God in prayer. Tell God that you no longer wish to continue in sin and ask Him to grant you repentance in these areas. Confess the sins to God is prayer specifically. Take as much time as you need—God literally has all the time in the world, and this is that important. (Side-note: Confession is not a one-time thing. Repentance takes time and is not completed until glory. You may want to keep a short list of sins and repent and confess daily.)

Finally, find someone mature in the faith. This could be someone in your small group or your leader if you are doing this study in a one-on-one setting. Set aside a time after completing this chapter where you share your biggest struggles, one-on-one. They will pray with you and support you as you seek repentance from God.

Leader Notes

The repentance chapter can be one of the most difficult. You have to maintain the tension between a heart of repentance that is part of the process of regeneration that God causes in the heart of the believer when you come to faith and a serious disposition towards sin. You have to give a lot of grace, but you also cannot make it seem like sin is not a big deal and we can just ignore sin.

A helpful analogy to use is that of Kingdoms. When someone comes to faith, they leave the Kingdom of the World and join the Kingdom of God. There is a new law written on their hearts, but old habits. As you acclimate to living in the Kingdom of God, you will more and more love God's ways and be able to live righteously, as God has called us to live.

Everyone going through this study needs to do the practicum. It's that important. Don't allow anyone to move forward without completing it. If you are doing this in a group setting, encourage people to pair up with more mature followers of Jesus for accountability. You don't need to be a one-on-one for every person. It is also highly recommended that accountability partners be the same gender.

10. THE HOLY SPIRIT

Purpose: To introduce the Holy Spirit and discuss what it is that the Spirit accomplishes in the life of the follower of Jesus.

Indwelling and Temple

The Holy Spirit is offered freely to those who earnestly wish to receive Him. The Spirit is not an ideological force, but the third person of the Trinity, and as such, literally indwells a person to influence said person. The Spirit is the seal or mark of King Jesus upon His people. Further, as the Holy Spirit indwells the follower of Jesus, the follower and, likewise, the church become the temple of God on earth and thus the Spirit purifies His temple in order to reside in and among us as the temple of God.

- Receiving the Spirit (Luke 11:13)
- Literal influence (Acts 2:3-4)
- The seal of the Spirit (2 Corinthians 1:22; Ephesians 1:13)
- You are the temple (1 Corinthians 6:19-20)
- The church is the temple (1 Corinthians 3:16)
- Purification of the temple (Titus 3:5)

Power of the Spirit

The Spirit of God is the power of God. The Spirit of God kept chaos at bay when the world was created and he continues to guard his beloved against chaos, specifically the powers of darkness in the cosmos. In this, the Spirit of God gives us hope to endure this life. He strengthens the inner man for perseverance and makes us bold witnesses of all that God has done in our world, which is entrenched in chaos.

- Keeping chaos at bay (Genesis 1:1-2)
- Hope (Romans 15:13; Galatians 5:5)
- Bold witness (Micah 3:8; Acts 1:8; Mark 13:11)
- Internal strength (Ephesians 3:16)

Work of the Spirit

The Holy Spirit works in us and in the world. He teaches us about Christ by reminding us of what we have read in the scriptures. The Spirit himself is a witness of what God has done in saving us and testifies to the Father, as well as to our own hearts, of who we have become in Christ. The Spirit connects us to God's will, because it is only the Spirit who knows the mind. Further the Spirit anoints and commissions us for God's calling. He unifies the holy ones of God for purpose of God's mission. And the Spirit brings us to a heart of repentance resulting in joyful obedience to God.

- To teach about Christ (John 14:26)
- The witness of the Spirit (Acts 5:32)
- To connect you to God's will (1 Corinthians 2:11)
- Anointing/Commissioning (Luke 3:21-22; Acts 13:2)
- Unification of the Saints (2 Corinthians 13:14)
- Obedience (Ezekiel 36:27)

Spiritual Gifts

Spiritual gifts are allotted to Christians by the Holy Spirit according to His own will and purposes. It is, however, admirable for one to desire gifts, especially gifts that edify the church and communicate the Good News of Jesus to the world around us. Gifts must always be exercised so as to build up and never to distract or destroy. This is especially the case with speech and communicatory gifts that are specifically designed for furthering the Kingdom of God.

- Allotment of gifts (1 Corinthians 12:4-11)
- Desire for gifts (1 Corinthians 12:31)
- Warning regarding gifts (1 Corinthians 13:1-4)
- Speech (Acts 4:31)
- Communicatory gifts (1 Corinthians 14:1, 9; 2 Peter 1:21)
- Appropriate use of gifts (Romans 12:6-8)

Practicum

Do a practicum on this lesson where you encourage your student or small group to take a spiritual gifts quiz or to use another discovery tool. Keep in mind, these tools are far from perfect and are more likely to produce results that accord with the individuals desires more than the persons actual gifting. But remember, desire is a factor in the Spirit's allocation of gifts. So if someone desires to be an evangelist and lacks the skill to do so, rather than discount their results as error, it may be that you should pray over the person to receive the Spirit's anointing for that calling and then train them and send them to practice the gifting to see if it is God's will for them. Talk through and share the results.

Leader Notes

Emphasize that the Holy Spirit's presence is the seal of one's salvation. Encourage the group to discuss ways that they have witnessed the Spirit of God working in their lives, either through gifting or through conviction of sin, or otherwise. If someone has not experienced the Spirit of God in an obvious way, encourage them to pray that God would demonstrate His power through His Spirit in their lives. Encourage them not to feel discouraged by a lack of understanding of the Spirit's presence as if that is a sign they are not saved—it is the presence of the Spirit that evidences salvation; not experiencing the presence of God may just be a sign of spiritual immaturity in some way and not a challenge to the persons salvation.

11. BAPTISM

Purpose: To establish a biblical basis for baptism that allows the student to understand the significance of what God has done in Spirit baptism as well as the significance of their submission to water baptism.

Jewish Baptism

There is not much to say about Jewish baptism from the scriptures, however, it appears that the act of baptism as a washing may stem from the healing that took place in the seven baptisms of 2 Kings 5. Baptism in the New Testament typifies proto-baptismal events of the Jewish people such as the baptism into the Red Sea that occurred when God rescued the Israelites from Egypt. Further, the tabernacle was baptized in the cloud that demonstrated the presence of the Lord in the tabernacle (so too does baptism today represent the indwelling of the Spirit of God in His temple—his people). Further, baptism was seen as a contractual commitment to repent of sins as is appropriate for any ceremonial washing.

- Washing for regenerative purposes (2 Kings 5:14)
- Baptized into God's provision (1 Corinthians 10:2; cf. Exodus 14:15-31; Numbers 9:15-22)
- Repentance (Luke 3:3; Acts 13:24, 19:4)

Baptism of the Holy Spirit

When a person has faith in Jesus as Lord and believes the good news about Jesus, the person gets baptized—so to speak—with the Holy Spirit. This is a reference to the indwelling and sealing of the Spirt from the previous lesson. In Christian baptism there is a change of focus from repentance from sins to following the Holy Spirit. The Spirit is referred to by fire, a symbol of power and energy. The power of God's Spirit causes rebirth, an immersion into the ways of Christ.

- Spirit falls on belief (Acts 11:15)
- Change of focus (Acts 1:5)
- Fire (Matthew 3:11)
- Immersion in Christ (Galatians 3:27)
- Rebirth (John 3:5)
- Be filled (Ephesians 5:18)

Christian Sacrament and Covenant

In the church, the practice of baptism as guarded as a sacrament, a holy thing. The act of baptism remembers Jesus' death and resurrection and reminds us that though we will one day die, we will also rise to new, eternal, and perfected life in God's Kingdom. Baptism rehearses the death and resurrection scenario to symbolically substantiate our belief in Jesus' death and resurrection and also our future hope of resurrection.

The sacrament remembers that spirit and water baptism are not the same. Water baptism is a commitment founded on a person's belief in the lordship of Jesus Christ. It is not a ceremonial washing that results in purification, but an act of obedience in response to the regeneration of the person by the Holy Spirit. We are baptized into Christ and thus baptism is the outward visible statement a Christian partakes in, in order to testify to their conversion and make commitments to Christ and his church.

- Symbolism (Colossians 2:12; Romans 6:3-10)
- Spirit and water baptism are not the same (Acts 10:47)
- Not just washing but loyalty to Christ (1 Peter 3:21)
- Baptism into Christ alone (1 Corinthians 1:11-16)
- Baptism marks true conversion (Acts 2:41)

Mode and Timing

Although it is clear that Spirit baptism occurs when a person believes, there are questions about mode and timing of the act of water baptism. Some hold that baptism does not require full immersion in water. The scriptures seem to testify that a large body of water was necessary or at least normative for baptism to occur.

Further, some believe that you can be baptized through water baptism into the covenant community of the church, however, it appears in scripture that the sacramental act of water baptism occurs after there is evidence of faith; Peter seems to suggest that the Gentile believers should be baptized only because they have already displayed evidence of conversion through the baptism of the Holy Spirit.

- Immersion (John 3:23; Colossians 2:12; Mark 1:5)
- Follows belief (Acts 10:44–48)

Leader Notes

At this point, you are going to want to have a serious conversation about baptism. In the Great Commission, Jesus commands us as disciples to baptize people. People are not commanded to be baptized. It's something the church does. If your student has not been baptized by immersion, on profession and understanding, it is a good idea to take the next step and move them towards baptism, even if, for some reason, they are hesitant.

In this lesson, help them to understand the roots of baptism in Judaism as an act of commitment. Then demonstrate to them the spiritual significance of the baptism of the Holy Spirit that has already occurred and then show them that their commitment to Christ requires they submit to water baptism as a mark of the future hope of eternity with Him.

12. THE CHURCH

Purpose: To introduce the form of the church as a body, the function of the church in worship and ministry, and the biblical governance of the church as a priesthood under qualified elders.

Fellowship

The scriptures describe a church that regularly meets together, not just on Sundays, but really living life among each other in community. This is necessary as Christ is present in our midst as we gather, even in small numbers. The body is therefore to be united and devoted to one another, not just a gathering of individuals.

- Regular Meeting (Hebrews 10:24-25)
- Spiritual Presence (Matthew 18:20)
- Devotion to One Another (Acts 2:42)
- Unity of the Body (Romans 12:4-5)

Corporate Worship

Corporate worship is the gathering of the local body of Christ to remember Christ through the celebration of the Lord's Supper, to worship through song, preaching/teaching, exhortation, reading of scripture, and prayer. Further, corporate worship is liturgical, that is orderly and intentionally designed to communicate truths to the people while lifting up praise and adoration to God.

- Music (Psalm 95:1, Ephesians 5:19, Hebrews 2:12, Colossians 3:16)
- Preaching (2 Timothy 4:1-2, Ezra 7:9-10, 1 Timothy 4:16, Nehemiah 8:8)
- Reading (1 Timothy 4:13, Romans 10:17, Hebrews 4:12, 2 Timothy 3:16-17)
- Prayer (Acts 1:14, 2 Corinthians 1:11, Ephesians 6:18, 1 John 5:14)
- The Lord's Supper (1 Corinthians 11:17–26)
- Intentionality/Orderliness (1 Corinthians 14:26–33)

Government and Role of Elders

Elders are overseers of the ministry of the church. They are not themselves the only ministers, but ought to set an example to the congregation as to how to serve/minister. The primary role of elders is to preach/teach the truth of God's word and to encourage the congregation to Christ-like living. Elders are pastors, or shepherds, who care for the body of Christ. As those who care for the church, Elders oversee the ministry of the church and have appropriate authority to do so.

- Preaching/Teaching (2 Timothy 4:2, 1 Timothy 3:2, Titus 1:9)
- Shepherding/Pastoring (Acts 20:28, Jeremiah 3:15, 1 Peter 5:1-3)

49

- Overseeing (Hebrews 13:17, Titus 1:7, Acts 14:23)
- Training for Ministry (Ephesians 4:11-12)

Democracy and Priesthood

There is a democratic element to church governance whereby the church body holds the elders accountable to their responsibility to the church and their biblical qualifications. United, the church is a priesthood, able to communicate corporately the will and purpose of Christ for his church.

- Congregational participation under the elders (Acts 15 [note: vv. 6, 12, 22])
- Appointment of ministry leaders under the elders' authority (Acts 6:1-6)
- Priestly activity of the united body (1 Peter 2:4-5)
- Ministerial efforts of the entire body (1 Corinthians 12 [note: vv. 11, 12, 24-25])
- Congregational discipline of elders (1 Timothy 5:19)

Ministry

The ministry of the church comes under the oversight of the elders but is executed by the congregation. Members of the church are to care for one another's needs as if they are their own needs, pray for one another, encourage one another, participate in disciple-making within the church body and outside the church body, and be involved in reaching out to those who do not know Jesus as Lord and Savior.

- Care for one another (John 13:34-35, Romans 12:10, 1 Peter 4:9)
- Meet the needs of one another (Philippians 2:4, Galatians 6:2, Acts 2:44-47)
- Pray for one another (Ephesians 6:18, James 5:16, Colossians 1:9)
- Encouragement (1 Thessalonians 5:11, Hebrews 10:24)
- Generosity/giving (2 Corinthians 9:7, 1 Chronicles 29:14, 2 Corinthians 9:8-11, 1 Timothy 5:17-18, Galatians 6:6, 1 Corinthians 9:4 [note: Today, the command to provide for the teachers of the church ought to extend to the full function of the church if the congregation wishes to have facilities and program as part of their church function.])
- Church discipline/restoration (Matthew 18:15-20, Titus 3:9-11, 1 Corinthians 5:11)
- Disciple-making (Matthew 28:19-20, Acts 1:8, Romans 10:14-15, John 15:16)
- Outreach (Matthew 25:35-40, James 1:27)

Leader Notes

Where there are guidelines in scripture for how a local church is to be structured and for the purpose of the local church, each local church body is going to be unique with variance in how it operates according to their understanding of the key scriptures on church function and governance. For this reason, you may want to read through the by-laws of the local church so that you will be able to talk about the scriptures in context of your local church. Also, make sure you are sensitive to those who have been a part of churches with different structures.

As you lead people through these scriptures, the leader needs to be intentional about emphasizing the need for every believer to be devoted to regular participation (not simply attendance) in corporate worship, regular attendance in small groups, and regular involvement of the ministry of the church. The church is its members, not simply its leaders, and thus the local church needs every single member to operate as God has intended.

13. CHURCH MEMBERSHIP

Purpose: To distinguish between the universal and local/visible church and to establish a basis for church membership.

Universal Church

The universal church is made up of all those who belong to Christ's Kingdom: past, present, and future. Local churches are made up of both believers who belong to the Kingdom and unbelievers who are present in the local body for other reasons than loyalty to Jesus Christ.

- The GREAT congregation (Hebrews 12:22–24)
- References to the universal church (Matthew 16:18, Ephesians 1:22, Colossians 1:18, Galatians 1:13, 1 Corinthians 10:32)
- Differentiating the local body from the universal (1 Corinthians 1:2)
- Unbelievers among believers (Matthew 13:24–30)

Practices that Require a Local Church

All of the practices of the church in Chapter 12 require a local body of believers in order to execute on a practical level. The existence of local churches in the New Testament is evidence that it was so even from the beginning. Even churches that are a part of organizations with a greater hierarchy need to have local bodies in order to carry out the practices and purposes of Christ's church. Other practices that we see in scripture are the pastoring of local congregations, ...

- Pastoring a local congregation (Acts 20:28)

- Supporting sister churches (1 Corinthians 16:1–3)

- Setting an example of faith for other churches (1 Thessalonians 1:7)

- Participation with other local churches (Romans 16:16)

Local Church Membership

The practice of Church Membership allows the elders of the church to know who is a part of the local covenant community in order is to carry out the purposes of the church in the lives of those people. Although the practice of church membership varies from church to church today, from the beginning of the church there was a process of determining who was in and who was out.

- Numbering of the congregation (Acts 1:15; 2:41, 47, 5:14)
- Summoning the church members (Acts 6:2)
- Joining a church (Acts 5:12-13)
- Baptism as an initiatory act of membership (Acts 2:37–41)
- Revoking church membership (1 Corinthians 5:13)
- Local body and small groups (Acts 2:46)

Leader Notes

Church membership is considered unbiblical in some circles for the ·
simple fact that there is not a single go-to verse to say that local
churches must have an institutional membership structure. But, like
much of our theology (for example, the Trinity), church membership,
while not explicit in a single text, is obvious in the scriptures.

Emphasize that the early church had a process to know who was in and
who was out of the local church. Each local church today has a different
process for membership, but virtually all local churches have a process
even if they don't realize it—the pastors know the people who they are
responsible for. In preparation, be sure to know what your church
requires of members and what the process is for becoming a member.

NOTE: At this point in the book, the student should be baptized or be
preparing for baptism. They should now see the importance of church
membership and should be encouraged to place membership in the
local church.

14. CHRISTIAN OBEDIENCE

Purpose: To demonstrate the power and necessity of obedience to Jesus for the Christian and to demonstrate the significance of the Lord's inevitable discipline.

Following the Law in the Old Testament

In the Old Testament, there was a written law. This law was an expression of God's heart as it was delivered to the people through the discernment of Moses and the prophets. The heart of the law is to treat others well, with mercy and humility, before God. Faithfulness to God is exhibited in the keeping of God's law and thus it is good to know God's law and to remember it. Righteousness and blessing flow from the Law in the Old Testament.

- Heart of the Law (Matthew 7:12; Micah 6:8)
- Faithfulness (Psalm 119:30)
- Know the Law (Joshua 1:8)
- Remembering the Law (Deuteronomy 6:6-7)
- Righteousness through the Law (Psalm 103:17-18)
- Blessing of the Law (Deuteronomy 30:16)

The Law in the New Testament

In the New Testament, we are called to fulfill the law of Christ by living according to God's Spirit, not the letter of the law. In this way, the letter of the OT law is obsolete. The NT law is a law of love: love for people and love for Jesus. Jesus has fulfilled the requirements of the OT law in his death and resurrection and thus we are free to carry out the heart of the law as reflected in the greatest commandments of God to love God and neighbor.

- Spirit (Romans 7:6)
- Obsolescence of the OT Law (Hebrews 8:13)
- Love as Law (Galatians 6:2)
- Love for Jesus (John 14:15)
- Jesus fulfills the OT Law (Matthew 5:17)
- The greatest law (Luke 10:27)

The Lord's Discipline

The scriptures call us to endure suffering as the means by which God disciplines us. Biblical discipline is discipline in the sense of training more so than punishment for wrongdoing. God is a Father who disciplines us to produce a harvest of righteousness in us. God also uses teachers to admonish us and the church body as a whole to discipline us. Admonition and discipline are good for those who wish to be wise and, thus, discipline is an expression of God's love.

- Suffering as discipline (Hebrews 12:7)

- Fatherly discipline (Hebrews 12:8-9)

- Product of discipline (Hebrews 12:10-11)

- Admonition of teachers (1 Thessalonians 5:12–13)

- Church discipline/restoration as God's discipline (Matthew 18:15-20)

- Goodness of discipline (Proverbs 12:1)

- Discipline as God's love (Revelation 3:19)

Obeying God

Jesus is Lord and thus there is an expectation that we obey him. If we say we believe in Jesus, but don't obey we do not in fact believe, because God has chosen us for obedience. The obedient know God's will, pray effectively, and have a strength that is foreign to the disobedient.

- The Lordship of Jesus (Luke 6:46)

- Deceiving yourself (James 1:22)

- God chose us for obedience (John 15:16)

- Reveals God's will (Romans 12:2)

- Effectiveness of Prayer (1 John 3:21-22)

- Strength of obedience (Matthew 7:24)

Leader Notes

Obedience is hard. Emphasize the necessity of obedience as well as the grace available for failure. Inspire obedience by highlighting the growth that takes place as we follow Jesus faithfully.

Although it is true that we will continue to struggle with sin until we are glorified, do not let that be an excuse for complacency in sin or giving up on repentance.

Be prepared to talk about the Old Testament law (or Torah). There was an expectation that the Jews of the OT times follow these laws to the T, but there was also grace in times of failure built into the law itself. Today, we have the Spirit of God and are not called to live according to every command of the OT, but according to the heart of the law revealed by the Spirit of God in us.

Also, be sure not to let this chapter be only about sin. There is a lot of crossover, but repentance is more about sin—the don'ts. Obedience is more about the dos. Encourage and brainstorm ways that you can proclaim your love for God by loving others in obedience to Jesus' commands.

15. PRAYER

Purpose: To emphasize the importance of prayer and equip God's people to be faithful in the ministry and discipline of prayer.

What is Prayer? How to Pray

In the simplest form, prayer is talking to God, just as you would talk to anyone else. The content of prayer is adoration for God's character, confession of sinfulness and sins, thanksgiving for what God has done, and asking. Asking can be described as supplication. Supplication is a humble entreating of God for the things needed, whether for yourself or for others (intercessory prayer). Prayer is Spirit-empowered and, as such, even when we don't have the right words to express what we mean in prayer to God, the Spirit of God interprets our prayers from our heart and prays for us.

- Talking to God (Jeremiah 29:12)
- Adoration of God (Matthew 6:9)
- Confession/forgiveness of sin (1 John 1:9; Psalm 32:5; Matthew 6:12-13)
- Thanksgiving to God (Colossians 3:17; Psalm 105:1)
- Supplication/Asking (1 John 5:15; 1 Chronicles 16:11; Matthew 6:10-11)
- Spirit-empowered (Romans 8:26)

'Rules' for Prayer

Prayers are effective when we ask according to God's will. We are to pray in any circumstance and all the time, regularly and faithfully. Prayer is not with lofty speech or sacred words and phrases, but in common language. We are to pray in confidence that God hears us, knowing, however, that our prayers are hindered by intentional sin and disobedience to God. Ancient people often prayed demonstrably (demonstrated prayer with their bodies) as a sign that they are not ashamed of God and that they are positionally in the place of submission to Him. And because we believe in the power of God, we pray for our rulers, that they would lead in a way that honors God.

- According to His will (1 John 5:14)
- In any circumstance (James 5:13)
- All the time (Colossians 4:2; 1 Thessalonians 5:17)
- Regularly/Faithfully (Romans 12:12)
- In normal words and speech (Matthew 6:7)
- Pray with confidence in God (Philippians 4:6)
- Obedience and prayer (Proverbs 15:8; Psalm 66:18)
- Pray demonstrably—shamelessly, positionally (1 Timothy 2:8)
- Remembering authorities (1 Timothy 2:1-2, cf. Romans 13)

Prayer Practicum

End this chapter with one of the following practicums.

1) Have the student and leader alike create a prayer journal. You can do this digitally or in a notebook. Make a page (or the cover) that has reminders about how and why to prayer. Use headings in the entries for the different types of prayers for each day: Adoration, Confession, Thanksgiving, Supplication. Fill out the first day and pray together through both prayer journals. Both the teacher and student should pray out-loud.

2) Create a spontaneous prayer guide. This could be on a bookmark, in the leaf of your Bible, or digitally on a desktop background. Decorate it with reminders about how and why to pray. Make headings for Adoration, Confession, Thanksgiving, and Supplication. Unlike in practicum 1, you don't need to write in specifics. But you should pray specifically, identifying exactly what you adore about God and exactly what sins you want forgiveness for, etc. Both student and teacher should pray out-loud through their prayer guides.

Leader Notes

As in the other practicums, don't skip it or relax on it. Prayer is such an important part of the Christian faith and many people are not effective in prayer because they simply do not know how to do it. Spend extra time with this if necessary and make sure the student knows how to pray effectively by the end.

Sample Prayer Guide

Adoration	Confession	Thanksgiving	Supplication (For me)	Intercession (For others)
God YOU ARE...	My SINS this week are...	I PRAISE God for...	WORK in my life...	Please HEAL...
God, YOU HAVE DONE...	God, FORGIVE me for...	I am THANKFUL for...	Give me STRENGTH for...	Please SAVE...
God, YOU HAVE PROMISED...	HELP me to be more...	My BLESSINGS are...	TEACH me to...	Please COMFORT...

16. EVANGELISM

Purpose: To demonstrate the need for both public and relational evangelism and to equip the student to participate in the evangelistic process.

Public Evangelism

The church has been commanded to make disciples of the nations. This is accomplished through the public ministries of testimony, reading of scripture, and preaching of the Good News of Jesus Christ. We are told to never stop speaking of what we have come to believe, and we are to proclaim the Good News of Jesus systematically to all the world.

Public evangelism takes two forms: direct and indirect. Direct evangelism is when you have an intentional conversation with someone about their sin and redemption offered through Jesus or when you publicly proclaim that message to a group of people. Indirect evangelism is living according to the precepts of the scriptures in such a way that others question your convictions. The logical defense of your actions is that Jesus is Lord and you are saved from wrath through him.

- Make Disciples (Matthew 28:18-20)
- Testimony (Acts 20:21)

- Public reading (1 Timothy 4:13; Romans 10:17)
- Preach the Word (2 Timothy 4:2)
- Never stop speaking (Acts 4:20)
- Systematic (Acts 1:8)

Relational Evangelism

Relational evangelism is the exposure people receive to Jesus and the Good News as a natural consequence of being in a relationship with a Christian, whether a friend, family member, coworker, neighbor, etc. Everyone has a close circle of about 8-15 people that they are in natural relationship with. You have an obvious evangelistic ministry to your own children, to friends and family, and to others you encounter on a regular basis in life. These relationships and others are providential, orchestrated by God, for the purpose that your testimony might lead them to the truth of Jesus Christ. Further, the way that you live is a testimony to others, but we must still use words to give a defense of the truth when the opportunity arises.

- To your kids (2 Timothy 1:5)
- To friends (Mark 5:19–20)
- Peer-to-peer (Mark 1:28)
- Providential relationships (Acts 17:26–27)
- Living righteously before others (Matthew 5:16)
- Ready to give a defense (1 Peter 3:15)

Roles in Evangelism

God chooses to work through his people to lead people into his Kingdom, but conversion is something God alone accomplishes.

- God brings the growth (1 Corinthians 3:7)
- Lord and workers (Matthew 9:38)
- Human proclamation (Romans 10:14-15)

Evangelism Practicum

The student should identify someone they want to share Jesus with. The teacher should help them prepare to meet with this person. Have the student setup a coffee or lunch appointment for the explicit purpose of sharing Jesus. Depending on the situation, it could be helpful if the student tells their friend or family member what the purpose of the meeting is up front. If the student will be more comfortable, the teacher can attend the meeting as well for support, but the student should do as much of the talking as possible. The student can share their own testimony of coming to Jesus or the student can engage in an apologetic approach, whichever is more appropriate for the situation.

If the friend wants to engage the conversation past the single meeting, setup another time to meet, invite them to church or small group, or whatever is best to follow up.

If the friend is ready to make a commitment to Christ, ask them if they would like to study the Bible with you and setup a time to begin taking them through this study from the beginning.

Leader Notes

Evangelism is messy and no two encounters are the same. Fruit in evangelism also differs from encounter to encounter. Don't allow the student to have false expectations of what God is going to do. Pray that he does great things, but let God be the bearer of fruit.

Make sure you and the student are thoroughly prepared for this task. You may even want to sharpen your own skills by making an appointment of your own before getting to the practicum.

17. Continued Spiritual Growth

Purpose: To introduce the student to the spiritual journey. A commitment to Christ is a very important landmark on the timeline of the Christian life, but the journey continues until the end comes. This requires intentionality and practice.

The Journey (Sanctification)

We are all on a spiritual journey. No one has arrived. The process of becoming Christ-like is sanctification (recall chapter 7). Faith in Jesus is the means of becoming more like him and progressing in your spiritual journey. Jesus makes you holy and will complete your spiritual journey when you are perfected in the end. We are called to mortify (kill) sin in our lives. As we are become more holy, God uses us for special purposes, even though we are not perfected until the end. On the journey we must constantly keep our minds focused on the words of Christ as the means by which we progress on our spiritual journey.

- Faith in Jesus (Acts 26:17–18)
- Jesus makes you holy (Hebrews 2:11)

- Process: Being made holy (Hebrews 10:14)
- God will complete his work (Philippians 1:6)
- Mortification (Colossians 3:5)
- Special purposes (2 Timothy 2:20–23)
- Complete sanctification as the goal (1 Thessalonians 5:23)
- Means of sanctification (John 17:17)

Spiritual Leadership

It is important to place yourself under spiritual leadership. This first means under the authority of the elders as already discussed in previous chapters. But it also means having someone to mentor you, to be a spiritual father or mother for you (1 Corinthians 4:15). Older men and women with more experience in their faith are commanded to teach the younger (Titus 2:1-8) so that all can grow in faith. Do you already have a spiritual mentor? Who can you ask to mentor you? For most, this cannot be the lead pastor of the church as he has all of the flock to care for. It could be a small group leader, someone who brought you to faith, or anyone else in the church with the spiritual maturity to lead, teach, and keep you accountable to Christ.

Spiritual Disciplines (Practices)

There is no exhaustive list of spiritual disciplines. A spiritual discipline is a practice that is spiritual in nature and which strengthens you spiritually. Spiritual disciplines ought to be a regular part of the life of the Christian, although they will look different in everyone's life. Other spiritual disciplines not mentioned might be solitude, study, service, sacrifice, and submission.

- Fasting (Matthew 4:2-4, 6:16-18; cf. Philippians 3:19)
- Giving (2 Corinthians 9:7, Malachi 3:10; Proverbs 11:24)
- Prayer (Hebrews 4:16)
- Physical fitness (Proverbs 23:21; 1 Corinthians 6:19-20, 9:27, 10:31, Ephesians 5:18)
- Fellowship (Acts 2:42)
- Worship (1 Chronicles 16:29)
- Truth-seeking (2 Timothy 3:16-17)
- Rest (Matthew 11:28, Genesis 2:3, Exodus 20:8-11)
- Celebration (Philippians 4:4, Ecclesiastes 5:18–19)

Intentionality

Read Philippians 3:12–16.

- Does spiritual maturity equal reaching the goal or perfection? Note the Apostle Paul claims to be spiritually mature (v. 15), but not perfect (v. 12).
- Is spiritual maturity something the Apostle Paul focuses on? How do you know? (v. 12)
- Does the Apostle Paul focus on past failures or on future glory? (v. 13)

70

- What is the Apostle Paul's goal on his spiritual journey? (v. 14)

- How does the Apostle Paul think that spiritually mature Christians should think? (v. 15)

- Regardless of how mature we are in Christ, what should we be intentional to live by? (v. 16)

Leader Notes

Be prepared to deal with the tension between sinner and saint (we are simultaneously sinners and holy at the same time). Encourage the student to try out various spiritual disciplines. Talk through fitness and diet practices. Maybe do a fast together. Ask about their giving habits, Sabbath (rest) habits, personal worship practice, etc.

18. HOW TO READ THE BIBLE

Purpose: To introduce the student to the tools necessary to read the Bible well.

Read the Big Story (Metanarrative)

Read Acts 6:8-7:60. Notice how Steven recaps the story of Jesus all the way back at Abraham. Matthew does the same thing at the beginning of his Gospel (Matthew 1). Look at the first verses of 1 Chronicles. The chronicler begins his story with Adam. Notice the Bible begins with creation in Genesis 1 and Adam in Genesis 2. And it ends with a perfect creation in Revelation 21-22. Even though the Bible is made of 66 books that are not all chronological, it is still—to quote the Bible Project (bibleproject.com)—One unified story that leads to Jesus.

Reading the Bible should be first and foremost an effort to read, understand, and know the story. Doctrine (teaching) and practice have a place but must be understood within the big story of the scriptures. In Acts 7, that is exactly what Stephen did. He told the big story and showed Jesus at the center of it all.

Look for Jesus (Read Christologically)

Read Luke 24:13–27. The risen Jesus walked with the disciples on the road and interpreted the Old Testament scriptures to them, demonstrating where he was present all throughout the scriptures. You may be reading the story and looking for the big story, but be stuck somewhere in the Old Testament, wondering what all this has to do with Jesus, heaven, the church today. It can seem irrelevant.

But Jesus was present all the way in the beginning and persists to the end. This whole story is wrapped in Jesus. If you can't see Jesus in the text, that's OK. Keep reading and keep searching. But, here's a few rules, places you can see Jesus clearly.

- In the law: The law shows us our inability to follow God in our own strength. When you read the law, you remember the mercy of God through Jesus Christ that bought us redemption at the cross.

- In the prophets: The prophets reflect the law, looking back to the sins of Israel and the sins of humankind. They also look forward to a future redemption of God's people, often specifically to the event of the birth, life, death, resurrection and lordship of Jesus Christ.

- In the Levitical system: The Levitical system lays the legal foundation for the necessity of Jesus's death in order to save us from the wrath of God due for our sins. In this way, the Levitical system shows us a shadow of Christ.

- In the LORD: When Jesus referred to himself as "Lord, Lord" (Matthew 7:22; Luke 6:46; Amos 3:13) he wasn't just referring to himself as a lord or even a new supreme Lord. He was alluding to the Hebrew phrase Adonai (lord) Yahweh (personal name of God) which are both translated as Lord (LORD=Yahweh). The very important phrase often translated Lord GOD in the Old Testament was quoted by Jesus in order to identify himself as the supreme LORD over all things. And the name LORD shows up all over the Old Testament. Particularly when the LORD shows up bodily, we are therefore to read the text as an appearance of Jesus in the Old Testament.

Read like the Original Reader

The Apostle Peter tells us that the writers of the scriptures wrote as they were carried along by the Holy Spirit. We believe that there is a divine oversight of the scriptures, but we also believe that "men wrote." That means that their own context, language, style, knowledge and education is all reflected in the writings.

There are a number of differences between our context and theirs. The ancient world was prescientific. That doesn't mean they were dumb—quite the opposite! But they didn't live by the scientific method so we can't force any text to speak into any scientific field. It wasn't what it was written for.

Another difference is worldview. We live in a world that sees a stark separation between the spiritual and physical worlds. But to the ancient reader there is very little separation between the spiritual and the physical. They lived in a world of spirits, ghosts, giants, gods, witches, shamans, and oracles. When you read of the spirit world in the scriptures, read it as though the original author and audience believed they were very real and active. Whether you believe they are is a question that belongs to theology, but you can't remove it from the big story even if you choose to disagree with it.

Read the Context (immediate, literary, historical, biblical)

Context is the set of circumstances that form the setting of a text that clarify the meaning. The **immediate context** is the first place to start. Never read a handful of words without understanding the surrounding text.

For example, when you read that, "I can do all things through him who strengthens me," (Philippians 4:13) it's tempting to read this to mean that you can literally do anything you dream of if you follow Jesus. But, notice there are keys in the context—the surrounding text—that govern the meaning of this text. It cannot be yanked from its context and a new meaning forced upon it. In context the Apostle Paul is speaking about how he has been able to endure difficult and blessed circumstances and persevered through it. Paul does not mean that he can win a basketball game, hike mount Everest, or get a promotion at work because of Jesus. He means that he can endure any circumstance because Christ strengthens him to endure.

The **literary context** is the second context to consider. Literary context refers to the form and function of the text. Consider what the purpose of the text is. Is it law? Is it poetry? If it's poetry, is it praise or wisdom? Or is it prophesy? Is it a narrative, part of a story? Is the story intended to be historical or is it an allegory?

These questions are important for a number of reasons. When you get to the Gospels and Jesus tells a parable, you know he is manufacturing a story to make a point. We can, because it's parable, forgive inconsistencies or illogical conclusions. But, if it's history, we need to believe what is written. If you are reading poetry of any kind it's going to be clouded in symbols, metaphors, and other figurative language. When you're reading law, it will most likely give real life details. You have to make these sorts of considerations in order to read the text well.

The **historical context** has to do with the place and time the story takes place. The biblical history is not the only history and frequently the biblical story is affected by what is happening in the world at large. The key to understanding many passages is to know the history of the ancient world. What is happening during this period of history? How will the writer and reader perceive the writing?

Finally, the **biblical context** is where you place the text into the greater story. You might not have all the story if you're new to reading the Bible. That's OK. Just like when you are doing a puzzle, you fit some pieces together and set them to the side, not knowing how they fit into the bigger picture, when you make connections to the Bible as a whole in a text, but you don't know how they work, you can hold them in tension. You can set them to the side, keeping them in clear view until you find the way to work them in later in your study. Keep reading and keep building the puzzle and you'll be well onto your way to understanding the big story of the Bible.

Leader Notes

Walk through the principles of reading the Bible with the student and work through examples of each in the text.

Remember that it takes time to really know the big story. Encourage the student to keep reading and keep working to grow in faith and understanding.

Made in the USA
Las Vegas, NV
06 January 2023

65130345R00049